TENUTA CASTELLO
SEDE E STABILIMENTO IN DESANA (VC)

RISO
SUPERFINO
ARBORIO

INGREDIENTI: RISO ARBORIO GARANTITO 100%

Produzione limitata

PESO NETTO / NET WEIGHT
POIDS NET / NETTO GEWICHT **1 kg** e

DA CONSUMARSI PREFERIBILMENTE ENTRO IL (vedi retro etichetta)

TENUTA CASTELLO
SEDE E STABILIMENTO IN DESANA (VC)

RISO
SUPERFINO
CARNAROLI

INGREDIENTI: RISO CARNAROLI GARANTITO 100%

MONDATO A MANO
SENZA USO DI DISERBANTI

Produzione limitata

PESO NETTO / NET WEIGHT
POIDS NET / NETTO GEWICHT **1 kg** e

DA CONSUMARSI PREFERIBILMENTE ENTRO IL (vedi retro etichetta)

LES PETITS PLATS
FRANÇAIS
SIMON & SCHUSTER
ILLUSTRATED

perfect risotto

LAURA ZAVAN

Photography by Marie-Pierre Morel

SIMON &
SCHUSTER
ILLUSTRATED

London · New York · Sydney · Toronto
A CBS COMPANY

English language edition published in Great Britain by
Simon and Schuster UK Ltd, 2011
A CBS Company

Copyright © Marabout 2004

SIMON AND SCHUSTER
ILLUSTRATED BOOKS
Simon & Schuster UK
222 Gray's Inn Road
London WC1X 8HB
www.simonandschuster.co.uk

1 2 3 4 5 6 7 8 9 10

Translation: Prudence Ivey
Copy editor English language: Nicki Lampon

Colour reproduction by Dot Gradations Ltd, UK
Printed and bound in U.A.E.

ISBN 978-0-85720-359-5

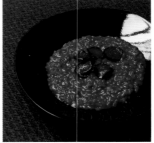

Contents

Risotto essentials

The very best risotto comes from the north of Italy in the regions of Piedmont, Lombardy and Venice. Why? Because that is where risotto rice is grown. Italy is the primary producer of rice in Europe: there are around 230,000 hectares of rice fields in northern Italy, on the Po plain, and especially in Piedmont and Lombardy. The rice grown there is almost entirely 'japonica', the only variety with which risotto is made.

Which rice to choose?

Risotto rice is rich in starch. This means that its grains bond together well, absorbing liquid but staying firm to the bite.

Carnaroli is the best risotto rice. Cooked for between 18–20 minutes it stays firm during cooking.

Vialone Nano is mostly grown and eaten in the Veneto region. It becomes 'all'onda' when cooked – soft with a loose texture that ripples down the plate when the plate is inclined. Cooked for 15–16 minutes, it holds its texture well when cooked.

Arborio rice is the best known variety outside Italy. It is cooked in 15–16 minutes but loses some bite.

How to serve risotto

In Italy, risotto is traditionally the 'primo piatto', served after the 'antipasto' (starter) and before the 'secondo piatto' (main course). For this type of serving 50–70 g (1¾–2½ oz) (equivalent to a good handful of dry rice) should usually be the right amount. You can also serve risotto as a main course, in which case you should increase the amount of rice correspondingly.

Hints and tips

The best risottos are made with seasonal produce.

Real homemade stock is the best. If you don't have any, use good quality stock cubes.

Buy Parmesan cheese in blocks of at least 200 g (7 oz). It will keep best in the fridge, wrapped in cling film. You can also use it on pasta, gratins, etc.

It's worth keeping a good supply of dried mushrooms, saffron, truffles, aromatic herbs, dried fruit and, of course, Parmesan cheese so that you can whip up a last minute risotto. See the recipes on pages 12–19 for inspiration.

Stock recipes

Vegetable stock
In a large saucepan, bring 2.5 litres (4½ pints) of water, 2 onions, 2 carrots, 2 celery sticks and 2 leeks to the boil. Season and leave to cook for 40 minutes over a medium heat. Strain. You could also add pea pods, asparagus off-cuts or whatever you have handy.

Chicken stock
Add a chicken (or its legs and wings only) to the vegetable stock ingredients. Cover with 2.5 litres (4½ pints) of water, bring to the boil, skim, then simmer for at least 1 hour 30 minutes. Strain and leave to cool, then skim the grease off.

Beef stock
Add 500 g (1 lb 2 oz) of braising steak on the bone to the vegetable stock ingredients. Cover with 2.5 litres (4½ pints) of water, bring to the boil, skim, then reduce the heat. Simmer for 2 hours on a very low heat. Season once cooked. Strain and leave to cool, then skim the grease off. Alternatively, you could freeze the cooking liquid from a meat stew if there are leftovers. This will work perfectly in a risotto.

Fish stock
In a pan, heat 50 ml (2 fl oz) of olive oil and add 2 finely chopped onions and 2 finely chopped leeks. Cook for 5 minutes. Add 500 g (1 lb 2 oz) of cleaned fish scraps, 1 bouquet garni and a few white peppercorns. Add 2.5 litres (4½ pints) of water, bring to the boil, skim, then cook for 30 minutes over a medium heat. Strain.

Shellfish stock
In a pan, heat 50 ml (2 fl oz) of olive oil and add 1 finely chopped onion, 1 finely chopped carrot and 1 finely chopped celery stick. Cook for 5 minutes. Add the cleaned heads and shells of the shellfish and 1 bouquet garni. Add 100 ml (3½ fl oz) of white wine, leave to evaporate, then add 2.5 litres (4½ pints) of water, bring to the boil, skim and cook for 30 minutes over a medium heat. Strain.

Stock cubes
You should always have a supply of vegetable, chicken and beef stock cubes to hand. These should be organic if possible and gluten free.

A basic risotto

Preparation time: 5 minutes
Cooking time: 25 minutes
Serves 6–8 people

1.5 litres (2¾ pints) beef, chicken
  or vegetable stock (see page 6)
2 tablespoons olive oil
1 onion, finely chopped
450 g (1 lb) risotto rice (Carnaroli,
  Arborio or Vialone Nano)
100 ml (3½ fl oz) dry white wine
  (or extra stock)
salt and freshly ground black pepper
50 g (1¾ oz) cold butter, cubed
60 g (2 oz) grated Parmesan cheese

Set the stock simmering on the hob.

In a heavy-based pan, heat the oil, add the onion and leave to cook gently for 5 minutes until soft and translucent.

Add the unwashed rice and stir for 2 minutes until all the ingredients are well combined. The rice will begin to stick to the bottom of the pan but make sure it does not brown. It should look translucent.

Add the wine (or stock) and allow to evaporate completely, stirring constantly.

Add a ladleful of stock. Continue cooking over a low heat for around 15 minutes (depending on the type of rice used) and adding a ladleful or two of stock once the last has been absorbed. Stir regularly. This method of cooking rids the rice grains of the layer of starch that forms around them and gives the risotto its unctuous consistency.

While cooking, add any additional ingredients (vegetables, meat, shellfish, etc). Check the consistency and season. The risotto should remain fluid and the grains of rice should stay firm. Add a little more stock if necessary.

Remove from the heat and add the cold butter and Parmesan, stirring in quickly. Cover and leave to rest for 2 minutes; this will make the risotto even more creamy.

Serve at once while hot. If you leave the risotto it will continue to cook in the pan and the texture will change irreparably.

A basic risotto (continued)

Tip: You can prepare the first steps of the risotto in advance – heat the onion and the rice in the oil, add the wine and evaporate, season and stop cooking – this is especially useful when you are cooking for guests.

Variation: With this base recipe you could make a risotto with prosecco or champagne. Add the wine (1 bottle) little by little, alternating with the stock for the duration of the cooking time.

Speedy: If you are pressed for time, cook the onion, then add the rice and three times its weight in stock all at once. Cook over a low heat in a covered pan for 15 minutes. The result is not bad but it's not a true risotto…

Saffron risotto

Preparation time: 10 minutes
Cooking time: 25 minutes
Serves 6

1.5 litres (2¾ pints) chicken or
  beef stock (see page 6)
2 tablespoons olive oil
1 onion, finely chopped
450 g (1 lb) risotto rice (Carnaroli
  or Arborio)
100 ml (3½ fl oz) dry white wine
salt and freshly ground black pepper
3 pinches of saffron
50 g (1¾ oz) cold butter, cubed
60 g (2 oz) grated Parmesan cheese

Set the stock simmering on the hob.

Heat the olive oil in a heavy-based
pan and cook the onion over a low
heat for 5 minutes.

Add the risotto rice and stir for
2 minutes until translucent.

Add the dry white wine and stir until
evaporated. Season.

Cook, adding the hot stock bit by bit
and stirring regularly.

After 12 minutes, add the saffron,
dissolved in a little stock.

Once cooked, remove from the heat,
add the butter and Parmesan and stir
well. Serve hot.

Mushroom and parsley risotto

Preparation time: 10 minutes +
  20 minutes soaking
Cooking time: 25 minutes
Serves 6

50 g (1¾ oz) dried mushrooms
  (e.g. porcini)
1.5 litres (2¾ pints) chicken or
  vegetable stock (see page 6)
2 tablespoons olive oil
1 onion, finely chopped
450 g (1 lb) risotto rice (Carnaroli
  or Arborio)
100 ml (3½ fl oz) dry white wine
salt and freshly ground black pepper
a small bunch of fresh flat leaf
  parsley, finely chopped
50 g (1¾ oz) cold butter, cubed
60 g (2 oz) grated Parmesan cheese

Place the dried mushrooms in a bowl,
cover with warm water and leave to
soak for 20 minutes. Drain and cut
into pieces.

Set the stock simmering on the hob.

Heat the olive oil in a heavy-based
pan and cook the onion and
mushrooms over a low heat for
5 minutes.

Add the risotto rice and stir for
2 minutes until translucent.

Add the dry white wine and stir until
evaporated. Season.

Cook, adding the hot stock bit by bit
and stirring regularly.

Once cooked, remove from the heat,
add the parsley, butter and Parmesan
and stir well. Serve hot.

White truffle purée and pine nut risotto

Preparation time: 5 minutes
Cooking time: 25 minutes
Serves 6

1.5 litres (2¾ pints) chicken
  or beef stock (see page 6)
2 tablespoons olive oil
1 onion, finely chopped
450 g (1 lb) risotto rice (Carnaroli
  or Arborio)
100 ml (3½ fl oz) dry white wine
salt and freshly ground black pepper
4 tablespoons pine nuts
25 g (1 oz) white truffle purée
50 g (1¾ oz) cold butter, cubed
60 g (2 oz) grated Parmesan cheese

Set the stock simmering on the hob.

Heat the olive oil in a heavy-based pan and cook the onion over a low heat for 5 minutes.

Add the risotto rice and stir for 2 minutes until translucent.

Add the dry white wine and stir until evaporated. Season.

Cook, adding the hot stock bit by bit and stirring regularly.

Meanwhile, toast the pine nuts in a dry pan until golden brown. Set aside.

Once cooked, remove the risotto from the heat and add the white truffle purée, butter and Parmesan. Stir well and serve hot with the toasted pine nuts sprinkled on top.

Balsamic vinegar and Parmesan risotto

Preparation time: 5 minutes
Cooking time: 25 minutes
Serves 6

1.5 litres (2¾ pints) chicken or
   vegetable stock (see page 6)
2 tablespoons olive oil
1 onion, finely chopped
450 g (1 lb) Carnaroli risotto rice
100 ml (3½ fl oz) dry white wine
salt and freshly ground black pepper
4 tablespoons traditional balsamic
   vinegar (see Tip), plus extra to
   serve
50 g (1¾ oz) cold butter, cubed
60 g (2 oz) grated Parmesan
   cheese, plus extra to serve

Set the stock simmering on the hob.

Heat the olive oil in a heavy-based pan and cook the onion over a low heat for 5 minutes.

Add the risotto rice and stir for 2 minutes until translucent.

Add the dry white wine and stir until evaporated. Season.

Cook, adding the hot stock bit by bit and stirring regularly.

Once cooked, remove from the heat, add the balsamic vinegar, butter and Parmesan and stir well. Serve hot, topped with shavings of Parmesan and a few drops of balsamic vinegar.

Tip: Traditional balsamic vinegar must have been aged for at least 12 months. If unavailable, you can reduce a normal, decent balsamic vinegar until it has a syrupy consistency.

Potato and rosemary risotto with lardo di colonnata

Preparation time: 15 minutes
Cooking time: 25 minutes
Serves 6

1.5 litres (2¾ pints) vegetable stock
  (see page 6)
200 g (7 oz) lardo di colonnata,
  cut into thin strips
300 g (10½ oz) potatoes, diced
1 onion, finely chopped
1 sprig of rosemary
350 g (12¼ oz) Vialone Nano
  risotto rice
100 ml (3½ fl oz) dry white wine
salt and freshly ground black pepper
30 g (1 oz) cold butter, cubed
60 g (2 oz) grated Parmesan cheese

Set the stock simmering on the hob.

Heat the lardo di colonnata over a low heat and cook the potatoes, onion and rosemary for 5 minutes.

Add the risotto rice and stir for 2 minutes until translucent.

Add the dry white wine and stir until evaporated. Season.

Cook, adding the hot stock bit by bit and stirring regularly.

Once cooked, remove from the heat, add the butter and Parmesan and stir well. Serve hot.

Tip: Lardo di colonnata is a cured pig fat. It is a Tuscan delicacy and can be found in specialist delis and online.

Rocket, smoked cheese and walnut risotto

Preparation time 10 minutes
Cooking time 25 minutes
Serves 6

1.5 litres (2¾ pints) beef stock
  (see page 6)
2 tablespoons olive oil
1 onion, finely chopped
450 g (1 lb) risotto rice (Carnaroli
  or Arborio)
100 ml (3½ fl oz) dry white wine
salt and freshly ground black pepper
150 g (5¼ oz) smoked scamorza,
  diced
20 walnuts, chopped
30 g (1 oz) rocket, chopped
30 g (1 oz) cold butter, cubed
40 g (1½ oz) grated Parmesan
  cheese

Set the stock simmering on the hob.

Heat the olive oil in a heavy-based pan and cook the onion over a low heat for 5 minutes.

Add the risotto rice and stir for 2 minutes until translucent.

Add the dry white wine and stir until evaporated. Season.

Cook, adding hot stock bit by bit and stirring regularly.

Once cooked, remove from the heat and add the scamorza, walnuts, rocket, butter and Parmesan. Stir well and serve hot.

Tip: Scamorza is similar to mozzarella and can be found in specialist delis and online. The smoked variety adds additional flavour.

Ginger and pomegranate risotto with a spice infusion

Preparation time: 10 minutes
Cooking time: 25 minutes
Serves 6

8 tablespoons herbs and spices,
  tied in muslin (see Tip)
15 g (½ oz) sea salt
2 tablespoons olive oil
1 onion, finely chopped
450 g (1 lb) risotto rice (Carnaroli
  or Arborio)
100 ml (3½ fl oz) dry white wine
salt and freshly ground black pepper
1 teaspoon grated fresh root ginger
40 g (1½ oz) cold butter, cubed
40 g (1½ oz) grated Parmesan
  cheese
seeds from 1 pomegranate,
  to serve

Bring 1.5 litres (2¾ pints) of water to the boil, add the bag of herbs and spices and simmer for 6 minutes. Add the salt, remove the bag and simmer over a low heat to keep warm.

Heat the olive oil in a heavy-based pan and cook the onion over a low heat for 5 minutes.

Add the risotto rice and stir for 2 minutes until translucent.

Add the dry white wine and stir until evaporated. Season.

Pour in 2 ladlefuls of the spiced water, add the ginger and cook, adding hot spiced water bit by bit and stirring regularly.

Once cooked, remove from the heat, add the butter and Parmesan and stir well. Serve hot, sprinkled with the pomegranate seeds.

Tip: Make your own spice infusion using a mixture of your favouite herbs and spices, tied in a small piece of muslin.

Prawn and herb risotto

Preparation time: 15 minutes
Cooking time: 25 minutes
Serves 6

1.5 litres (2¾ pints) vegetable stock
    (see page 6)
2 tablespoons olive oil
1 onion, finely chopped
450 g (1 lb) risotto rice (Carnaroli
    or Arborio)
100 ml (3½ fl oz) dry white wine
salt and freshly ground black pepper
a bunch of fresh herbs (e.g. parsley,
    chervil, tarragon, basil, coriander
    or mint), finely chopped
18–24 cooked shelled prawns,
    chopped
40 g (1½ oz) cold butter, cubed
20 g (¾ oz) grated Parmesan
    cheese

Set the stock simmering on the hob.

Heat the olive oil in a heavy-based
pan and cook the onion over a low
heat for 5 minutes.

Add the risotto rice and stir for
2 minutes until translucent.

Add the dry white wine and stir until
evaporated. Season.

Cook, adding hot stock bit by bit and
stirring regularly.

Once cooked, remove from the heat,
add the herbs, prawns, butter and
Parmesan and stir well. Serve hot.

Risotto primavera

Preparation time: 30 minutes
Cooking time: 40 minutes
Serves 6

1.5 litres (2¾ pints) vegetable
   stock (see page 6)
6 tablespoons olive oil
1 onion, finely chopped
400 g (14 oz) Vialone Nano
   risotto rice
100 ml (3½ fl oz) dry white wine
salt and freshly ground black pepper
250 g (8¾ oz) fresh peas
100 g (3½ oz) French beans, cut
   into very short lengths
2 baby carrots, diced
3 artichoke hearts, cut into eighths
250 g (8¾ oz) courgettes, chopped
350 g (12¼ oz) asparagus, cut into
   short lengths
5 sprigs of fresh parsley, finely
   chopped
50 g (1¾ oz) butter
60 g (2 oz) grated Parmesan cheese

Set the stock simmering on the hob.

Heat 4 tablespoons of oil in a large, lidded, heavy-based pan and cook the onion over a low heat for 5 minutes.

Add the rice and stir constantly with a wooden spoon over a high heat until translucent.

Add the wine, keep stirring until evaporated then season.

Add a ladleful of very hot stock then the peas, beans and carrots. Continue to cook over a low heat, adding more stock as it is absorbed.

Meanwhile, heat the remaining oil in a pan and cook the artichokes and courgettes for 2–3 minutes. Season and set aside.

Bring a small pan of water to the boil and cook the asparagus spears for 2 minutes. Set aside.

About 3 minutes before the rice is done, add the artichokes, courgettes and asparagus and heat through.

Remove the risotto from the heat, add the parsley, butter and Parmesan and stir in quickly. Cover and allow to rest for 2 minutes then serve.

Asparagus risotto with mascarpone

Preparation time: 30 minutes
Cooking time: 25 minutes
Serves 6

1 kg (2 lb 4 oz) asparagus, cut into
  short lengths
30 g (1 oz) butter
salt and freshly ground black pepper
1.5 litres (2¾ pints) vegetable stock
  (see page 6)
2 tablespoons olive oil
1 onion, finely chopped
450 g (1 lb) Vialone Nano risotto rice
100 ml (3½ fl oz) dry white wine
80 g (2¾ oz) mascarpone
80 g (2¾ oz) grated Parmesan
  cheese

Set the asaragus tips aside. Melt 20 g (¾ oz) of the butter over a low heat and cook the asparagus stalks for 2–3 minutes. They should remain crunchy. Season.

Bring a small pan of water to the boil and cook the asparagus tips for 2 minutes. Drain and cook in the remaining butter for a further minute. Set aside.

Set the stock simmering on the hob.

Heat the olive oil in a large, lidded, heavy-based pan and cook the onion over a low heat for 5 minutes.

Add the rice and stir constantly with a wooden spoon over a high heat until translucent.

Add the wine, keep stirring until evaporated then season.

Add the stock, ladle by ladle, stirring from time to time. After 10 minutes, add the asparagus stalks.

Once cooked, remove the risotto from the heat, add the mascarpone, asparagus spears and Parmesan, season with freshly ground black pepper and stir in quickly. Cover and allow to rest for 2 minutes before serving.

Variation: This risotto is also delicious made with white asparagus. Cook the tips and stalks (cut into 1 cm/½ inch pieces) in the stock for 2–3 minutes then add to the risotto halfway through cooking.

Risi e bisi

Risi e bisi (rice and peas) is a classic Venetian dish. Traditionally made on feast days, it is best prepared with freshly shelled peas when they are in season.

Preparation time: 30 minutes
Cooking time: 45 minutes
Serves 6

1.5 litres (2¾ pints) chicken or
  vegetable stock (see page 6)
400 g (14 oz) shelled fresh peas,
  pods reserved
60 g (2 oz) butter
2 onions, finely chopped
60 g (2 oz) pancetta, cut into pieces
400 g (14 oz) Vialone Nano risotto
  rice
salt and freshly ground black pepper
1 tablespoon chopped fresh parsley
60 g (2 oz) grated Parmesan cheese

Bring the stock to the boil in a large saucepan and cook the pea pods in the stock to add flavour to the risotto. Remove the pods and discard.

Melt 20 g (¾ oz) of the butter in a large, lidded, heavy-based pan and cook the onions and pancetta over a low heat for a few minutes.

Add the rice and cook for 2 minutes so that it picks up the flavour and becomes translucent.

Add the peas and a ladleful of stock and cook until the stock is absorbed.

Continue to add stock little by little as it is absorbed. Cook over a low heat, stirring occasionally. Season.

Remove the risotto from the heat and add the parsley, remaining butter and Parmesan. Check the seasoning. Cover for 2 minutes before serving 'all'onda' (see page 4).

Tips: You could blend the cooked pea pods and add them to the stock. The risotto will then be a lovely fresh green colour.

The smallest fresh peas cook very quickly so only add them 5 minutes before the rice is cooked.

Artichoke risotto

Preparation time: 15 minutes
Cooking time: 30 minutes
Serves 6

10 small purple artichokes
juice of 1 lemon
4 tablespoons olive oil
1 garlic clove, finely chopped
salt and freshly ground black pepper
1.5 litres (2¾ pints) chicken stock
  (see page 6)
2 shallots, finely chopped
450 g (1 lb) Vialone Nano risotto rice
100 ml (3½ fl oz) dry white wine
1 tablespoon chopped fresh flat
  leaf parsley
60 g (2 oz) cold butter
80 g (2¾ oz) grated Parmesan
  cheese

Wash the artichokes and remove and discard the hard outer leaves. Cut off the tips of the inner leaves and trim the stem, leaving about 2.5 cm (1 inch). Remove any tough green parts of the stem. Soak the artichokes in the lemon juice to prevent discolouring.

Halve the artichokes and remove the hairly choke from the hearts using a spoon. Finely slice the artichoke halves.

Heat 2 tablespoons of the oil and cook the artichokes and garlic for 5 minutes. They should be crunchy. Season.

Set the stock simmering on the hob.

Heat the remaining oil in a large, lidded, heavy-based pan and cook the shallots gently for 5 minutes.

Add the rice and stir constantly with a wooden spoon over a high heat until translucent.

Add the wine, keep stirring until evaporated then season.

Add the stock, ladle by ladle, stirring from time to time. After 10 minutes, add the artichokes.

Once cooked, remove the risotto from the heat, add the parsley, butter and Parmesan and stir in quickly. Cover and allow to rest for 2 minutes before serving.

Mushroom risotto

Preparation time: 1 hour
Cooking time: 40 minutes
Serves 6

1 kg (2 lb 4 oz) fresh mushrooms
(ceps, girolles, chanterelles, etc.)
5 tablespoons olive oil
90 g (3 oz) butter
2 garlic cloves, 1 left whole and
1 finely chopped
salt and freshly ground black pepper
2 tablespoons chopped fresh
parsley
1.5 litres (2¾ fl oz) chicken stock
(see page 6)
3–4 shallots, chopped
400 g (14 oz) Carnaroli risotto rice
100 ml (3½ fl oz) dry white wine
80 g (2¾ oz) grated Parmesan
cheese

Clean the mushrooms by plunging them into cold water a couple of times then dry. Cut the larger ones into pieces.

In a non stick pan, heat 1 tablespoon of oil and 10 g (¼ oz) of butter with the whole clove of garlic. Add one-third of the mushrooms (or one variety if using several types) and cook on a high heat until all their liquid is cooked off. Season, stir, reduce the heat and cook for a further 2–3 minutes. Repeat with the remaining mushrooms, adding more oil and butter each time.

Mix all the mushrooms together, remove the garlic, add the parsley and keep warm.

Set the stock simmering on the hob.

Heat the remaining oil in a large, lidded, heavy-based pan and cook the shallots and chopped garlic gently for 5 minutes.

Add the rice and stir over a high heat for 2 minutes without browning.

Add the wine and stir until evaporated. Season. Add the hot stock bit by bit, stirring from time to time.

After 10 minutes of cooking add the mushrooms. Check the seasoning.

Once the risotto is cooked (allow around 18–20 minutes), remove from the heat, add the remaining butter and the Parmesan, stir in, cover and leave to rest for 2 minutes before serving.

Variation: You could also use dried or frozen mushrooms for this recipe (cook them without defrosting).

Beetroot risotto

Preparation time: 30 minutes
Cooking time: 30 minutes
Serves 6

500 ml (18 fl oz) beetroot juice
1.5 litres (2¾ fl oz) vegetable stock
   (see page 6)
3 tablespoons olive oil
3 shallots, finely chopped
400 g (14 oz) Carnaroli or Arborio
   risotto rice
100 ml (3½ fl oz) dry white wine
2 cooked beetroot, peeled and
   blended
1 raw beetroot, peeled and finely
   sliced
salt and freshly ground black pepper
40 g (1½ oz) cold butter
40 g (1½ oz) grated Parmesan
   cheese

Pour the beetroot juice into a saucepan and reduce by half over a low heat. Keep warm.

Set the stock simmering on the hob.

Heat 2 tablespoons of oil in a large, lidded, heavy-based pan and cook the shallots over a low heat for 4–5 minutes.

Add the rice and stir over a high heat until translucent.

Add the wine, stir until evaporated, then add a ladleful of simmering stock. Stir.

Continue cooking over a medium heat, stirring regularly and adding the stock little by little as it is absorbed by the rice. After 10 minutes, add the blended beetroot to thicken the risotto and the beetroot juice, in stages.

Meanwhile, cook the raw beetroot slices quickly in a pan with the remaining oil. Season and keep warm.

Once the risotto is cooked (around 18 minutes), remove from the heat, add the butter and Parmesan and stir in. Cover and leave to rest for 2 minutes.

Serve decorated with a few slices of the sliced beetroot.

Heirloom vegetable risotto

Preparation time: 30 minutes
Cooking time: 30 minutes
Serves 6

200 g (7 oz) chervil roots (see Tip)
200 g (7 oz) parsley roots (see Tip)
200 g (7 oz) parsnips
200 g (7 oz) yellow beetroot
  (see Tip)
1.5 litres (2¾ pints) vegetable
  or chicken stock (see page 6)
4 tablespoons olive oil
salt and freshly ground black pepper
1 onion, finely chopped
400 g (14 oz) Carnaroli or Arborio
  risotto rice
100 ml (3½ fl oz) dry white wine
40 g (1½ oz) cold butter
40 g (1½ oz) grated Parmesan
  cheese

Wash and peel all the vegetables and add the peelings to the stock. Set the stock simmering on the hob.

Setting aside the long pointed ends of the root vegetables and a few slices of beetroot, slice the vegetables into 3 mm (⅛ inch) rounds.

Fry the sliced vegetables in 2 tablespoons of olive oil for 3 minutes. Season.

Brown the remaining vegetables and set aside to use as decoration. Strain the peelings from the stock.

Heat the remaining oil in a large, lidded, heavy-based pan and cook the onion over a low heat for 5 minutes.

Add the rice and stir over a high heat for 2 minutes until translucent.

Add the wine, stir until evaporated, add a ladleful of simmering stock, mix well and add the sliced vegetables.

Continue cooking over a medium heat, stirring regularly and adding the stock little by little as it absorbs.

Once the rice is cooked (allow around 15–18 minutes), remove from the heat, add the butter and Parmesan and stir in. Cover and leave to rest for 2 minutes. Serve, topped with the remaining vegetables.

Tip: These are heirloom vegetables not commonly found in supermarkets. You may be able to find them at farmers' markets, or try growing them yourself. Alternatively, you can use vegetables that are more widely available.

Pumpkin risotto

Preparation time: 20 minutes
Cooking time: 30 minutes
Serves 6

300 g (10½ oz) pumpkin, peeled,
  de-seeded and diced
3 tablespoons olive oil
70 g (2½ oz) butter
1.5 litres (2¾ pints) chicken stock
  (see page 6)
2 shallots, finely chopped
300 g (10½ oz) Vialone Nano
  risotto rice
100 ml (3½ fl oz) dry white wine
salt and freshly ground black pepper
500 g (1 lb 2 oz) pumpkin purée
  (see Tip)
2 pinches of grated nutmeg
2 pinches of ground cinnamon
80 g (2¾ oz) grated Parmesan
  cheese

Brown the diced pumpkin in a pan
for 2 minutes with 1 tablespoon of
olive oil and 20 g (¾ oz) of butter.
Set aside.

Set the stock simmering on the hob.

Heat the remaining oil in a large,
lidded, heavy-based pan and cook
the shallots over a low heat for
4–5 minutes.

Add the rice and stir over a high heat
for 2 minutes until translucent,
without allowing it to brown.

Add the wine, stir until evaporated,
add a ladleful of simmering stock,
mix well and season. Add the diced
pumpkin.

Continue cooking over a medium
heat, stirring regularly and adding
the stock little by little.

After 10 minutes, add the pumpkin
purée and spices.

Once the rice is cooked (allow around
16 minutes), remove from the heat,
add the remaining butter and the
Parmesan and stir in. Check the
seasoning, cover and leave to rest
for 2 minutes.

Tip: Choose a pumpkin that weighs
1.2 kg (2 lb 12 oz). To make the purée,
cut into large pieces and steam until
tender, around 15 minutes. Blend
(including the skin if organic).

Variation: Away from the heat,
add 2 tablespoons of mostarda de
Cremona and 2 amaretti biscuits,
blended together. Mostarda de
Cremona is an Italian condiment
consisting of candied fruit preserved
in a mustard flavoured syrup.

Radicchio risotto

Preparation time: 25 minutes
Cooking time: 30 minutes
Serves 6

800 g (1 lb 11 oz) radicchio
4 tablespoons olive oil
70 g (2½ oz) butter
4 shallots, finely chopped
200 ml (7 fl oz) red wine
salt and freshly ground black pepper
1.5 litres (2¾ pints) beef or
   vegetable stock (see page 6)
400 g (14 oz) Vialone Nano
   risotto rice
80 g (2¾ oz) grated Parmesan
   cheese

Cut off most of the root of the radicchio, leaving 1–2 cm (½–¾ inch), then peel off the outer leaves. Divide into four lengthways. Wash, dry and set a few leaves aside for decoration. Cut the remainder into 3 cm (1¼ inch) pieces.

Heat 2 tablespoons of oil and 20 g (¾ oz) of butter in a pan and cook half the shallots for 3 minutes over a low heat. Add the radicchio and sauté for 1 minute over a high heat.

Add half the red wine, allow to evaporate off, season and cook over a medium heat for a few more minutes. The radicchio should remain crunchy. Set aside.

Set the stock simmering on the hob.

Heat the remaining oil in a large, lidded, heavy-based pan and cook the remaining shallots over a low heat for 5 minutes.

Add the rice, increase the heat and cook for around 2 minutes until translucent.

Add the remaining wine, keep stirring until evaporated then season. Add a ladleful of hot stock and continue cooking over a medium heat, adding the stock little by little as the rice absorbs it, stirring as you go.

After 10 minutes cooking, add the warm radicchio and mix well.

Once the risotto is cooked (allow around 10 minutes), remove from the heat, add the remaining butter and the Parmesan, stir in, cover and leave to rest for 2 minutes. Decorate with the raw radicchio leaves.

Fennel and ricotta risotto

Preparation time: 15 minutes
Cooking time: 40 minutes
Serves 6

3 fennel bulbs, cut into quarters
  and leafy shoots set aside
4 tablespoons olive oil
salt and freshly ground black pepper
1 onion, finely chopped
400 g (14 oz) Vialone Nano risotto
  rice
100 ml (3½ fl oz) dry white wine
40 g (1½ oz) cold butter
50 g (1¾ oz) grated Parmesan
  cheese
200 g (7 oz) ricotta, to serve

Bring 2 litres (3½ pints) of water to the boil and add all but two quarters of the fennel. Cook until tender. Remove the fennel from the water with a slotted spoon and cut into small pieces. Keep the water simmering to use in the risotto.

Fry the two reserved quarters of fennel in 2 tablespoons of oil for 2–3 minutes then season. They should remain crunchy. Set aside to use for decoration.

Heat the remaining oil in a large, lidded, heavy-based pan and cook the onion over a low heat for 5 minutes.

Add the rice, increase the heat and cook for 2 minutes until translucent.

Add the wine, stir until evaporated, then add a ladleful of the hot fennel cooking water along with the boiled fennel.

Continue cooking for 15 minutes over a medium heat, stirring constantly and gradually adding more water as it is absorbed.

Check the seasoning and remove from the heat. Add the butter and Parmesan and stir in quickly.

Cover and leave to rest for 2 minutes then serve 'all'onda' (see page 4), decorated with a spoonful of ricotta, some of the fried fennel and the leafy fennel shoots.

Taleggio risotto with hazelnuts

Preparation time: 15 minutes
Cooking time: 20 minutes
Serves 6

100 g (3½ oz) hazelnuts
1.5 litres (2¾ pints) vegetable
  stock (see page 6)
2 tablespoons olive oil
1 onion, finely chopped
400 g (14 oz) Carnaroli risotto rice
100 ml (3½ fl oz) dry white wine
salt and freshly ground black pepper
leaves from 2 fresh sprigs of
  rosemary
300 g (10½ oz) taleggio, cut
  into pieces
40 g (1½ oz) cold butter
40 g (1½ oz) grated Parmesan
  cheese

Preheat the oven to 180°C (fan oven 160°C), Gas Mark 4 and toast the hazelnuts for a few minutes until golden. Alternatively, dry fry in a frying pan. Set aside to cool then remove their skins with your fingers and roughly chop.

Set the stock simmering on the hob.

Heat the oil in a large, lidded, heavy-based pan and cook the onion for 5 minutes over a low heat.

Add the rice and stir for 2 minutes over a high heat until translucent, without allowing it to change colour.

Add the wine and keep stirring until evaporated. Season and add the rosemary. Add the hot stock little by little, stirring constantly.

Once the risotto is cooked (allow around 16–18 minutes), remove from the heat, add the taleggio and check the seasoning.

Add the butter, Parmesan and half the hazelnuts. Mix well, cover and leave to rest for 2 minutes.

Serve, sprinkled with the remaining hazelnuts.

Variation: Taleggio is a strong cow's milk cheese from the region of Lombardy in Italy. You could replace it with Vacherin Mont d'Or.

Tomato and basil risotto

Preparation time: 25 minutes
Cooking time: 25 minutes
Serves 6

5 tablespoons olive oil
1 kg (2 lb 4 oz) very ripe plum
  tomatoes, skinned, de-seeded
  and chopped
1 garlic clove, crushed
salt and freshly ground black pepper
a bunch of fresh basil, a few leaves
  reserved and the remainder
  chopped
1.5 litres (2¾ fl oz) chicken or
  vegetable stock (see page 6)
1 onion, finely chopped
450 g (1 lb) Carnaroli or Arborio
  risotto rice
12–18 cherry tomatoes
60 g (2 oz) cold butter
60 g (2 oz) grated Parmesan cheese

Heat 2 tablespoons of olive oil in a pan and brown the plum tomatoes for 2 minutes with the garlic. Season and add half the chopped basil. Set aside.

Set the stock simmering on the hob.

Heat 2 tablespoons of oil in a large, lidded, heavy-based pan and cook the onion over a low heat for 5 minutes.

Add the rice and stir for 2 minutes over a high heat until translucent.

Add a ladleful of hot stock then add the plum tomatoes. Mix well. Add the stock little by little as the previous spoonful is absorbed by the rice.

Meanwhile, fry the cherry tomatoes in the remaining oil for 1 minute over a high heat. Keep warm.

After 16–18 minutes, when the rice is still al dente, remove from the heat then add the butter, Parmesan and remaining chopped basil. Leave to rest for 2 minutes.

Decorate with the cherry tomatoes and the reserved basil leaves.

Pear and Gorgonzola risotto

Preparation time: 20 minutes
Cooking time: 25 minutes
Serves 6

3 pears
30 g (1 oz) cold butter
1.5 litres (2¾ pints) chicken or
  vegetable stock (see page 6)
2 tablespoons olive oil
1 onion, finely chopped
1 celery stick, finely chopped
450 g (1 lb) Carnaroli or Arborio
  risotto rice
100 ml (3½ fl oz) dry white wine
200 g (7 oz) Gorgonzola, cut into
  pieces
freshly ground black pepper
60 g (2 oz) mascarpone
40 g (1½ oz) grated Parmesan
  cheese

Cut six attractive slices of pear to decorate and flash fry them in a knob of butter for 1 minute on each side. Keep warm.

Peel the remaining pears and cut into small pieces.

Set the stock simmering on the hob.

Heat the oil in a large, lidded, heavy-based pan and cook the onion and celery over a low heat for 5 minutes.

Add the rice and stir for 2 minutes over a high heat until translucent.

Add the wine and stir until evaporated. Add the hot stock little by little as each spoonful is absorbed by the rice.

Once the risotto is ready (allow around 18 minutes), add the Gorgonzola and chopped pear. Season with freshly ground black pepper and stir well.

Remove from the heat, add the mascarpone and Parmesan, cover and leave to rest for 2 minutes. Serve topped with the fried pear slices.

Tip: Gorgonzola is a blue cheese made in the Lombardy region of Italy. It's best to choose a ripe creamy version.

Variation: You could also add walnuts or hazelnuts.

Melon and lemon risotto

Preparation time: 20 minutes
Cooking time: 25 minutes
Serves 6

1 ripe melon (around 1 kg/2 lb 4 oz)
70 g (2½ oz) butter
1½ onions, finely chopped
1.5 litres (2¾ pints) chicken or
  vegetable stock (see page 6)
2 tablespoons olive oil
400 g (14 oz) Carnaroli or Arborio
  risotto rice
3 tablespoons marsala or port
salt and freshly ground black pepper
grated zest of 1 lemon
50 g (1¾ oz) grated Parmesan
  cheese

Cut the melon in half and remove the seeds. With a medium-sized spoon, make melon balls and scrape the remaining fruit from the skin.

Heat 20 g (¾ oz) of butter in a frying pan and cook one-third of the onions over a low heat. Add the melon balls and cook for 1 minute. Set aside.

Set the stock simmering on the hob.

Heat the oil in a large, lidded, heavy-based pan and cook the remaining onions and melon over a low heat for 5 minutes.

Add the rice and stir over a high heat for 2 minutes until translucent.

Add the marsala or port and stir until evaporated. Add a ladleful of hot stock, stir and season. Continue adding the stock gradually as it is absorbed by the rice, cooking over a low heat for around 18 minutes.

Remove the risotto from the heat, check the seasoning and add the melon balls, lemon zest, remaining butter and Parmesan. Mix well, cover and leave to rest for 2 minutes before serving.

Tip: To make a faster version of this risotto, cut the melon into small pieces and add directly to the risotto 3 minutes before you finish cooking.

Variation: Replace the melon with the chopped flesh of 2 mangoes, added around 4 minutes before you finish cooking.

Strawberry risotto

Preparation time: 15 minutes
Cooking time: 20 minutes
Serves 6

500 g (1 lb 2 oz) very juicy
   strawberries
1.5 litres (2¾ pints) vegetable
   or chicken stock (see page 6)
2 tablespoons olive oil
20 g (¾ oz) butter
1 onion, finely chopped
450 g (1 lb) Vialone Nano risotto rice
100 ml (3½ fl oz) dry white wine
salt and freshly ground black pepper
80 g (2¾ oz) mascarpone
80 g (2¾ oz) grated Parmesan
   cheese

Cut the strawberries into quarters, saving the 12 smallest for decoration.

Set the stock simmering on the hob.

Heat the oil and butter in a large, lidded, heavy-based pan and cook the onion over a low heat for 5 minutes, without allowing it to colour.

Add the rice and stir for 2 minutes until translucent.

Add the wine and stir well. Once it has evaporated, add the stock little by little as each spoonful is absorbed by the rice. Season.

After the rice has been cooking for 10 minutes, add the quartered strawberries.

Once the rice is cooked (after around 16 minutes), remove from the heat, add the mascarpone and Parmesan, stir and cover for 2 minutes. Serve decorated with the remaining strawberries, cut into little pieces.

Variation: You could replace the strawberries with raspberries or blueberries.

Courgette risotto with fried mullet

Preparation time: 30 minutes
Cooking time: 30 minutes
Serves 6

6 small mullet (around 1 kg/
 2 lb 4 oz) or 12 small mullet fillets
500 g (1 lb 2 oz) small courgettes,
 diced
1 garlic clove
leaves from 3–4 sprigs of fresh
 thyme
5 tablespoons olive oil
salt and freshly ground black pepper
1.5 litres (2¾ pints) fish stock
 (see page 6)
1 onion, finely chopped
400 g (14 oz) Carnaroli or Arborio
 risotto rice
100 ml (3½ fl oz) dry white wine
60 g (2 oz) cold butter
30 g (1 oz) grated Parmesan cheese

Fillet the fish, keeping the heads
and large bones for fish stock (you
can get your fishmonger to do this).
Remove the smallest bones with
a pair of tweezers.

Fry the courgettes, garlic clove and
thyme leaves in 2 tablespoons of oil
for 3 minutes. Season and discard the
garlic clove. Set aside.

Set the stock simmering on the hob.

Heat 2 tablespoons of oil in a large,
lidded, heavy-based pan and cook the
onion over a low heat for 5 minutes.

Add the rice and stir for 2 minutes
until translucent.

Add the wine and stir until
evaporated. Continue cooking, adding
the hot stock little by little as it is
absorbed by the rice and stirring
regularly.

Meanwhile, heat the remaining oil
in a non stick frying pan and cook
the fish fillets, skin side down, over
a high heat for 1 minute. Set aside
and keep warm.

After 10 minutes of cooking the
risotto, add the fried courgettes.

Once the risotto is cooked (allow
around 18 minutes), turn off the heat
and add the butter and Parmesan.
Stir, then cover and leave to rest
for 2 minutes.

Serve the risotto on warmed plates,
topped with 2 mullet fillets.

Tip: You can use frozen fish fillets
but defrost before frying.

Prawn and mushroom risotto

Preparation time: 40 minutes
Cooking time: 35 minutes
Serves 6

18–24 raw prawns (fresh or frozen
   and defrosted)
5 tablespoons olive oil
salt and freshly ground black pepper
1 kg (2 lb 4 oz) fresh cep
   mushrooms, cleaned and sliced
1 garlic clove, crushed
1.5 litres (2¾ pints) shellfish or
   fish stock (see page 6)
1 onion, finely chopped
450 g (1 lb) Carnaroli or Arborio
   risotto rice
100 ml (3½ fl oz) dry white wine
30 g (1 oz) cold butter
30 g (1 oz) grated Parmesan cheese

Shell the prawns and remove their heads (you can use these to make the stock). Cut half the prawns into two or three pieces.

Heat 1 tablespoon of oil in a pan and fry the prawn pieces for 1 minute. Season and set aside.

Fry the mushrooms and garlic in 2 tablespoons of oil over a high heat. You may need to do this in batches. Season and keep warm.

Set the stock simmering on the hob.

Heat the remaining oil in a large, lidded, heavy-based pan and cook the onion over a low heat for 5 minutes.

Add the rice and stir for 2 minutes over a high heat until translucent.

Add the wine and stir until evaporated, then add a ladleful of simmering stock. Mix well then add three-quarters of the mushrooms.

Continue cooking, adding hot stock little by little as it is absorbed by the rice and stirring regularly.

After 10 minutes, add the fried prawns. Check the seasoning.

Remove the risotto from the heat and add the butter and Parmesan. Stir, then cover and leave to rest for 2 minutes.

Just before serving, fry the whole prawns. Serve the risotto on warmed plates, topped with the remaining mushrooms and the whole prawns.

Langoustine risotto

Preparation time: 45 minutes
Cooking time: 50 minutes
Serves 6

18–24 fresh langoustines
4 tablespoons olive oil
salt and freshly ground black pepper
1 onion, finely chopped
400 g (14 oz) Carnaroli risotto rice
100 ml (3½ fl oz) dry white wine
grated zest of 1 lemon
60 g (2 oz) cold butter
30 g (1 oz) grated Parmesan cheese

Langoustine stock
2 tablespoons olive oil
1 carrot, peeled and chopped
1 onion, chopped
1 celery stick, chopped
2–3 sprigs of fresh parsley, basil
  or thyme
2 litres (3½ pints) water
100 ml (3½ fl oz) dry white wine
black peppercorns
salt and freshly ground black pepper

If using fresh langoustines, remove the shells and heads but keep the tails attached. Cut each into several pieces.

For the stock, cook the langoustine heads and shells over a high heat with the oil, vegetables and herbs.

Add the wine and water and a few peppercorns. Bring to the boil and leave to simmer for 30 minutes, skimming frequently. Strain, season and return to a gentle simmer.

Heat 2 tablespoons of oil in a large, lidded, heavy-based pan and cook the onion over a low heat for 5 minutes.

Add the rice and stir for 2 minutes over a high heat until translucent.

Add the wine and stir until evaporated, then add a ladleful of simmering stock.

Continue cooking, adding hot stock little by little as it is absorbed by the rice and stirring regularly. Season and add the lemon zest.

Meanwhile, fry the langoustine pieces in the remaining oil for 1 minute. Season and keep warm.

Once the rice is cooked (allow around 18 minutes), remove from the heat, add the butter and Parmesan and half the langoustine pieces. Stir, cover and leave to rest for 2 minutes.

Serve on warmed plates, topped with the remaining langoustine pieces.

Tip: If you cannot find fresh langoustines, use ready-prepared frozen ones and replace the langoustine stock with shellfish or fish stock (see page 6).

Squid ink risotto

Preparation time: 15 minutes
Cooking time: 35 minutes
Serves 6

6 tablespoons olive oil
600 g (1 lb 5 oz) squid, cleaned,
    tentacles reserved and half the
    body cut into rings
1 garlic clove, crushed
200 ml (7 fl oz) dry white wine
salt and freshly ground black pepper
1.5 litres (2¾ pints) vegetable
    or fish stock (see page 6)
1 onion, finely chopped
450 g (1 lb) Vialone Nano risotto rice
50 g (1¾ oz) squid ink
30 g (1 oz) cold butter
20 g (1¾ oz) grated Parmesan
    cheese

Heat 2 tablespoons of oil in a frying pan and brown the squid rings with the garlic over a hot heat. Add half the white wine, allow to evaporate, season and set aside.

Set the stock simmering on the hob.

Heat a further 2 tablespoons of oil in a large, lidded, heavy-based pan and cook the onion over a low heat for 5 minutes.

Add the rice and stir for 2 minutes over a high heat until translucent.

Add the remaining wine and stir until evaporated, then add a ladleful of simmering stock. Mix well and add the fried squid rings.

Continue cooking, adding hot stock little by little as each spoonful is absorbed by the rice and stirring regularly.

After 10 minutes, add the squid ink, diluted in a little hot stock.

Meanwhile, heat the remaining oil in a frying pan and brown the whole squid and the tentacles over a high heat. Season.

Once the rice is cooked (allow around 16 minutes), remove from the heat and add the butter and Parmesan. Stir, cover and leave to rest for 2 minutes.

Serve the risotto on warmed plates, topped with the whole fried squid and tentacles.

Tip: Squid ink is available from selected fishmongers.

Seafood risotto

Preparation time: 1 hour
Cooking time: 50 minutes
Serves 6

1 kg (2 lb 4 oz) mussels, cleaned
500 g (1 lb 2 oz) clams or cockles,
  cleaned
200 ml (7 fl oz) dry white wine
2 garlic cloves, crushed
½ a bunch of fresh parsley, chopped
1 litre (1¾ pints) fish stock
  (see page 6)
70 g (2½ oz) butter
500 g (1 lb 2 oz) raw prawns
  (fresh or frozen), shelled and
  heads removed
salt and freshly ground black pepper
2 tablespoons olive oil
1 onion, finely chopped
450 g (1 lb) Vialone Nano risotto rice
30 g (1 oz) grated Parmesan cheese

Put the mussels and clams or cockles in a large saucepan with half the wine, half the garlic and the parsley and cook over a high heat until the shells open.

Remove the flesh from the shells (keeping around 20 in the shells for decoration) and set aside in a little of the strained cooking liquid. Add the rest of the strained liquid to the stock.

Heat 20 g (¾ oz) of butter in a frying pan and cook the prawns over a high heat. Season.

Set the stock simmering on the hob.

Heat the oil in a large, lidded, heavy-based pan and cook the onion and remaining garlic over a low heat for 5 minutes.

Add the rice and stir for 2 minutes over a high heat until translucent, without allowing it to brown.

Add the remaining wine and stir until evaporated, then add the hot stock little by little as each spoonful is absorbed by the rice, stirring regularly.

Once the risotto is nearly cooked, add the seafood. Check the seasoning and adjust if necessary.

Remove from the heat and add the remaining butter and Parmesan. Stir, then cover and leave to rest for 2 minutes.

Serve 'all'onda' (see page 4), topped with the reserved shellfish.

Variation: You can use any seafood that is in season or available.

Saffron risotto cakes with scallops

Preparation time: 40 minutes +
2 hours chilling
Cooking time: 50 minutes
Serves: 6–8

3 pinches of saffron
1.9 litres (3¼ pints) vegetable
stock (see page 6)
60 g (2 oz) butter
20 g (1 oz) plain flour
200 ml (7 fl oz) single cream
4 tablespoons olive oil
1 onion, finely chopped
400 g (14 oz) Carnaroli risotto rice
100 ml (3½ fl oz) dry white wine
60 g (2 oz) grated Parmesan cheese
12 scallops (or more if required)
salt and freshly ground black pepper

Mix the saffron with 100 ml (3½ fl oz) of stock and leave to infuse. Bring a further 300 ml (10 fl oz) of stock to a simmer.

Melt 40 g (1½ oz) of butter in a saucepan, add the flour and whisk together until smooth. Heat for 2 minutes then add the hot stock and the cream, whisking to make sure no lumps form.

Add the saffron stock and cook over a low heat for 20 minutes. Leave to cool – the sauce should be quite thick.

Set the remaining stock simmering on the hob.

Heat 2 tablespoons of oil in a large, lidded, heavy-based pan and cook the onion over a low heat for 5 minutes.

Add the rice and stir for 2 minutes over a high heat until translucent.

Add the wine and stir until evaporated, then add the hot stock little by little, stirring regularly.

Cook for 14 minutes – the risotto should be very dense.

Remove the risotto from the heat and add 6 tablespoons of saffron sauce and the Parmesan. Spread the risotto on a baking tray lined with greaseproof paper and leave to cool.

Once cool, press into 6–8 ramekin dishes and set aside in the fridge for 2 hours.

Brown the risotto discs in a frying pan with the remaining oil or bake in a preheated oven at 200°C (fan oven 180°C), Gas Mark 6, until both sides are crisp and golden.

Cook the scallops in a frying pan with the remaining butter for 2–3 minutes. Season. Gently reheat the saffron sauce.

Serve the risotto discs with the scallops on a pool of hot saffron sauce.

Smoked eel risotto

Preparation time: 10 minutes
Cooking time: 25 minutes
Serves 6

8 tablespoons Lapsang Souchong
  tea leaves (or other smoked tea)
2 tablespoons rock salt
2 tablespoons olive oil
1 large onion, finely chopped
450 g (1 lb) Carnaroli risotto rice
salt and freshly ground black pepper
150–200 g (5¼–7 oz) smoked eel
  fillet, sliced
30 g (1 oz) butter
20 g (¾ oz) grated Parmesan
  cheese
4 tablespoons soy sauce
1 teaspoon honey

Bring 1.5 litres (2¾ pints) of water to the boil, add the tea leaves and set aside to infuse for 5 minutes. Strain.

Season with rock salt and keep on the heat without boiling.

Heat the oil in a large, lidded, heavy-based pan and cook the onion over a low heat for 5 minutes. Add the rice and stir for 2 minutes over a high heat until translucent.

Add a ladleful of tea, season and stir. Cook for around 15 minutes over a medium heat, adding the tea little by little as each spoonful is absorbed by the rice and stirring regularly.

Check the seasoning and adjust if necessary. Remove from the heat and add half the eel slices, the butter and Parmesan. Stir then cover and leave to rest for 2 minutes.

Meanwhile, heat the soy sauce and honey in a frying pan until syrupy, add the remaining eel slices and cook for 30 seconds.

Serve the hot risotto topped with the soy eel slices.

Tip: Smoked eel can be found in specialist fishmongers and certain supermarkets.

Chicken and vegetable risotto

Preparation time: 30 minutes
Cooking time: 40 minutes
Serves 6

1.5 litres (2¾ pints) vegetable stock
  (see page 6)
4 skinless chicken thighs
2 tablespoons olive oil
2 onions, finely chopped
2 carrots, peeled and finely
  chopped
2 celery sticks, finely chopped
400 g (14 oz) Vialone Nano risotto
  rice
100 ml (3½ fl oz) dry white wine
salt and freshly ground black pepper
40 g (1½ oz) cold butter
60 g (2 oz) grated Parmesan cheese
a few fresh sage or parsley leaves
  or sprigs of rosemary, to garnish

Bring the stock to a gentle simmer, add the chicken thighs and leave to poach for 15 minutes. Remove the chicken and set aside to cool. Leave the stock simmering on the hob.

Remove the chicken meat from the bones and cut into small pieces. Set aside.

Heat the oil in a large, lidded, heavy-based pan and cook the onions, carrots and celery over a low heat for 5 minutes.

Add the rice to the vegetables and stir over a high heat for 2 minutes until translucent.

Add the wine and stir until evaporated, then add a ladleful of hot stock, mix well and add the chicken.

Continue cooking for 15 minutes, adding the stock little by little as it is absorbed by the rice, stirring regularly.

Check the seasoning, remove from the heat and add the butter and Parmesan. Stir then cover and leave to rest for 2 minutes. Serve 'all'onda' (see page 4), garnished with the herbs.

Arancini

Preparation time: 1 hour + 2 hours
  chilling + overnight
Cooking time: 1 hour
Serves 6

500 ml (18 fl oz) vegetable stock
  (see page 6)
2 tablespoons olive oil
1 onion, finely chopped
200 g (7 oz) Arborio risotto rice
salt and freshly ground black pepper
a pinch of saffron
50 g (1¾ oz) grated Parmesan
  cheese
100 g (3½ oz) mozzarella, cut into
  pieces
50 g (1¾ oz) plain flour
200 g (7 oz) breadcrumbs
vegetable oil, for frying

Ragù

1 tablespoon olive oil
20 g (¾ oz) onion, finely chopped
20 g (¾ oz) carrot, peeled and finely
  chopped
20 g (¾ oz) celery stick, finely
  chopped
300 g (10½ oz) minced beef
salt and freshly ground black pepper
30 ml (1 fl oz) red wine
200 g (7 oz) canned tomatoes
1 bouquet garni
60 g (2 oz) peas
20 g (¾ oz) butter

Prepare the ragù a day in advance. Heat the oil in a large lidded pan and cook the onion, carrot and celery for 2–3 minutes. Add the beef and cook until it begins to colour and stick to the pan. Season. Add the wine and allow to evaporate. Add the tomatoes and bouquet garni, stir, cover and cook over a low heat.

After 30 minutes, add the peas and cook for a further 30 minutes until the ragù has thickened and the liquid has evaporated. Remove from the heat, remove the bouquet garni and add the butter. Leave to cool then set aside in the fridge overnight.

The next day, set the stock simmering on the hob.

Heat the oil in a large, lidded, heavy-based pan and cook the onion over a low heat for 5 minutes.

Add the rice and stir for 2 minutes over a high heat until translucent.

Add the hot stock little by little, stirring regularly. Season. Cook for 14 minutes, then add the saffron, Parmesan and 30 g (1 oz) of blended ragù. The risotto should be very dense. Keep warm.

With wet hands, take a handful of risotto and place it in the palm of your hand. Make a well in the centre of the rice and fill with a little ragù (about 30 g/1 oz) and a piece of mozzarella. Roll the rice into a ball around the ragù centre. Repeat with the remaining risotto and ragù, place on a baking tray and leave to chill in the fridge for 2 hours.

Mix the flour with 100 ml (3½ fl oz) of water and roll the risotto balls in the batter then in the breadcrumbs.

Heat the oil to 180°C/350°F in a high sided saucepan and fry 1–2 risotto balls at a time until golden (they should not touch the bottom of the pan). Drain on kitchen towel and eat while hot.

Sausage and leek risotto

Preparation time: 30 minutes
Cooking time: 30 minutes
Serves 6

4 tablespoons olive oil
3 leeks, sliced
salt and freshly ground black pepper
300 g (10½ oz) good quality
  sausages, skinned
1.5 litres (2¾ pints) vegetable stock
  (see page 6)
1 onion, finely chopped
450 g (1 lb) Carnaroli or Vialone
  Nano risotto rice
100 ml (3½ fl oz) dry white wine
30 g (1 oz) cold butter
60 g (2 oz) grated Parmesan cheese

Heat 2 tablespoons of oil in a pan over a high heat and fry the leeks for a few minutes. They should remain crunchy. Season and set aside.

Add the sausages to the pan and fry for a few minutes, breaking them up with a fork. Pour away the grease and set the meat aside.

Set the stock simmering on the hob.

Heat the remaining oil in a large, lidded, heavy-based pan and cook the onion over a low heat for 5 minutes.

Add the rice and stir for 2 minutes over a high heat until translucent, without allowing it to brown.

Add the wine and stir until evaporated, then add a ladleful of stock. Mix well and add half the leeks and all the sausages.

Continue cooking over a medium heat, stirring and adding the hot stock little by little as each spoonful is absorbed by the rice.

Once the risotto is cooked (around 16–18 minutes), remove from the heat and add the butter and Parmesan. Stir, then cover and leave to rest for 2 minutes.

Serve hot, topped with the remaining leeks.

Chicken liver and red onion risotto

Preparation time: 20 minutes
Cooking time: 30 minutes
Serves 6

70 g (2½ oz) butter
3 tablespoons olive oil
6 chicken livers, cut into large
  pieces
150 ml (3½ fl oz) marsala or
  dessert wine
salt and freshly ground black pepper
1.5 litres (2¾ fl oz) chicken stock
  (see page 6)
3 red onions, finely sliced
4–5 sprigs of fresh thyme or sage
  leaves, finely chopped
400 g (14 oz) Carnaroli risotto rice
80 g (1¾ oz) grated Parmesan
  cheese

Melt 20 g (¾ oz) of butter in a pan with 1 tablespoon of oil and cook the chicken livers quickly (make sure they do not overcook and become tough – they should still be pink in the middle). Add the marsala, leave to evaporate and season. Set aside.

Set the stock simmering on the hob.

Heat the remaining oil in a large, lidded, heavy-based pan and cook the onions and herbs over a low heat for 5 minutes. Set aside a few of the cooked onions for decoration.

Add the rice to the pan and stir for 2 minutes until translucent. Add the hot stock little by little as each spoonful is absorbed by the rice, stirring often.

After 10 minutes of cooking, add the chicken livers. Check the seasoning.

Once the risotto is cooked (allow around 10 minutes), remove from the heat, add the remaining butter and Parmesan, cover and leave to settle for 2 minutes before serving.

Serve decorated with the reserved onions.

Variation: In Venice, chicken liver risotto often includes giblets, sautéed in butter, added at the same time as the rice.

Index